Crocheted Trims

These delightful samples of baskets and cupid show a very popular practice of intricate embroidery designs with crocheted trim. Many of the patterns from the 1920s thru the 1930s called for the addition of crocheted designs to adorn the edge of a runner and enhance the theme of the item.

This was especially true with pillowcases where the lovely lass pictured had a skirt of lacy double crocheted lace.

cupid pattern on pages 22-23
rose bouquet in a black vase pattern on page 24
pansies in a fan basket pattern on page 25

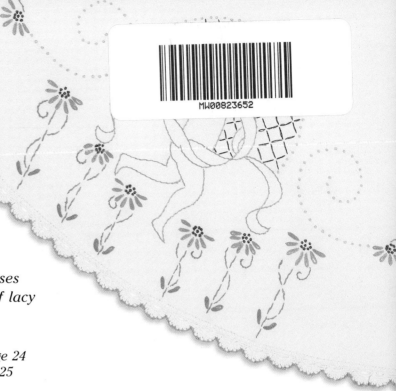

HELPFUL HINT
See Embroidery Stitches on pages 61 and 62.

Elegant Table Runners

My mother's home was always kept
As neat as neat could be,
The bureaus and the tables there
Wore stitched embroideries!

She said it was to save the wood
And keep the dust away,
I can't but think the pictures there
Helped pass the time away!

That when she went about her day
Her eyes could always find,
The pictures that her needle wrought,
A little peace of mind.

flowery mailbox pattern on page 28
donkey and cart pattern on page 31
vintage boot pattern on page 29
pitcher and bowl pattern on pages 30

Flowery Bygones

This quartet of stitched lovelies gives a good sampling of the favorite items that accompanied flowers on embroidered linens: ribbons, fans, umbrellas and, last but not least, the bouquet. The ribbons complement the flower arrangements, adding a lovely grace and flow to designs.

Bouquets were more common in days gone by and, unfortunately, have been relegated to proms and weddings today; but the lasses of yore were comfortable toting these around for no reason at all!

Another item that is now just a memory or prop in a play is the fan. When women wore much tighter undergarments and "foundation" pieces than we are used to these days, fans helped many a light-headed woman maintain her poise on hot summer days! It's a pity this beautiful decorative accessory has gone by the wayside.

"His" pattern on pages 39
spray pattern on page 32
parasol pattern on page 33
fan pattern on pages 34-35

Sweet Dreams

Many women today have great collections of embroidered linens. Whether passed down from mothers and grandmothers or discovered at a flea market or garage sale, stitched treasures are hard to resist. While amassing these stitches is a sport unto itself, many women need ideas for displaying and sharing their treasures.

One great way of getting their favorites out in the open is to make them into pillows. Pillows work in almost any decor and are an easy project. The only challenge is to get the most out of the embroidery by positioning the design over the pillow layout. Add a little embellishment with buttons, trim or lace and you have a lovely vintage treasure.

This pillow has a happy lot –
To make you comfy, like as not;
And when it aids your hours of ease,
Think kindly of the donor, please!
NEEDLECRAFT (March 1930)

heart and roses
patterns on page 38

basket and bows
pattern on page 37

tiny basket
pattern on page 40

bowl of lilacs
pattern on page 36

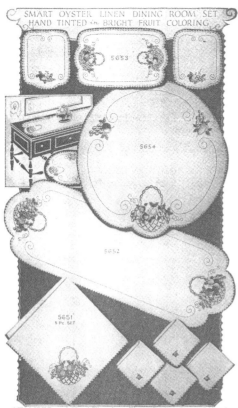

This page, from a 1926 Bucilla Needlework is an example of the fascination with baskets.

You have our hearts,
Our rosy wishes,
You have our hopes
In tiny stitches.

MODERN PRISCILLA
(June 1929)

Bonny Baskets

Baskets are found everywhere in fancywork and embroidery catalogs from the 1880s to the present. Every catalog had an extensive selection of flower filled baskets to choose from.

beribboned basket pattern on pages 42-43
blue flower bouquet pattern on page 41

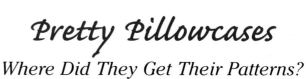

Pretty Pillowcases

Where Did They Get Their Patterns?

1890 – 1920: From the end of the 19th Century through the first decades of the 20th Century, catalogs and magazines were a major source of embroidery designs.

Patterns were available in both iron-on and perforated formats. The perforated designs were pinned to material and a brush or sponge was used to force powder or blueing (a mild bleach) through the holes. MODERN PRISCILLA, NEEDLE-CRAFT, MCCALL'S, BUTTERICK, LADIES' HOME JOURNAL and THE DELINEATOR were all magazines or publications which had mail-order sections or catalogs. Pre-stamped linens were also a popular item.

1920 - 1930: The 1920s saw a great expansion in the quantity and variety of needlework sources. "Fancywork", as decorative needlework was termed, became available in kit format from companies such as Bucilla and Frederick Herrschners. Publishers like McCall's and Butterick offered separate and extensive embroidery catalogs. It was a wonderful time for needleworkers with both a renaissance of colonial decorative arts as well as an explosion of highly stylized art deco and modern themes.

1930 – 1940: The 1930s and the Depression saw a continued interest in needlework but the variety of embroidery publications and catalogs dwindled a bit. Magazines such as MODERN PRISCILLA and NEEDLECRAFT (changed to NEEDLE ARTS) declined and disappeared by the end of the 30's and early 40's. Large chain and department stores took up some of the slack with their own lines of embroidery goods. Woolworths, Kresge's and JC Penney all had needlework departments and their own series of patterns. Newspapers began running quilting and needlecraft designs including some wonderful embroidered quilt series by artists such as Ruby McKim.

1940 – 1950: World War II put a crimp in the supply of materials available for needlework items. The variety of publications in general dwindled with paper rationing and the embroidery sector was not spared. NEEDLE ARTS and MODERN PRISCILLA disappeared. After the war, pattern houses such as Colonial Pattern Company (Aunt Martha's) and Vogart offered lines of embroidery transfers available through the mail and in department and dime stores. Colonial Pattern also continued THE WORKBAS-KET, begun in the late 1930s. This publication was a project sheet with all accompanying directions and transfers needed.

good luck pattern on pages 50-51, kitty pattern on pages 44-45, flower wreath pattern on pages 48-49

1950 - 1970: Interest in embroidery waned during this period. Vogart and Aunt Martha's were the two main pattern lines available in dime stores. Mail order catalogs like Herrschners and Lee Ward's were mainstays for crafters but featured a variety of crafts with embroidery making up a small part of their offerings.

1970 - Present: Enthusiasm for America's past and the Bicentennial created a resurgence of interest in historic handicrafts, including embroidery and quilting.

Commercial sources for embroidery designs were scarce and many women kept the interest in older patterns alive by setting up trading circles or "round robins". These were groups of women trading copies of old transfers and quilting patterns amongst themselves.

In the 1980s a surging interest in quilting, antiques and old linens started a small mail order offering of pattern reprints. After collecting linens, women became interested once again in creating their own keepsakes. Although quilting and cross stitch magazines, patterns and shops became popular, decorative embroidery or "fancywork" is just now coming into its own again. Linens are once again becoming important in home decorating.

*cornucopia pattern
on pages 56-57
hearts and flowers pattern
on pages 52-53
roses pattern on pages 46-47
flowers and bows pattern
on pages 52-53
purple wreaths pattern
on pages 46-47*

Stitching Thoughts

You have our hearts,
Our rosy wishes,
You have our hopes
In tiny stitches.
        MODERN PRISCILLA
            (June 1929)

Terrific Linen Runners

Linen runners look terrific draped across a chair or dresser. Or wrap one around a pillow shape then stitch up the sides to make a decorator pillow.

basket of lilacs pattern
on pages 54-55

darling deer pattern
on pages 48-49

magnolias pattern
on pages 56-57

Embellished Pockets to Hold Accessories

A delightful array of specialized holders and containers were very popular from the turn of the century until the 1940s. It harkens back to the saying:

"A place for everything and everything in its place".

From silverware to hair utensils, various items found elaborate embroidered sleeves and pockets created just for them. Few women today have either the time or the inclination to pamper combs and brushes!

comb and brush pattern on pages 58-59
grapes pattern on pages 60-61
star flower pattern on page 64
acorns and oak leaves pattern on pages 62-63

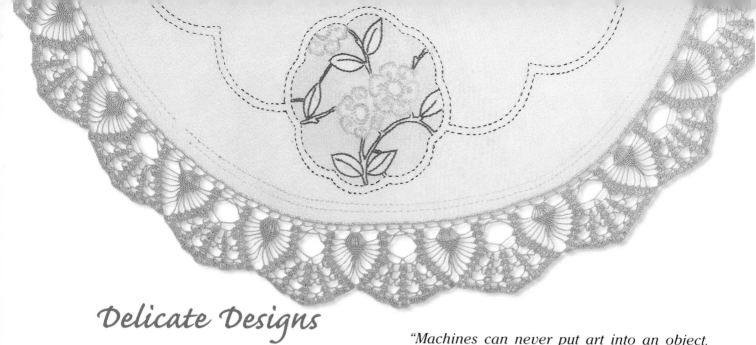

Delicate Designs

Surely the items pictured here show the truth in these words. Only the personal touch of a woman's hand can lend charm to this trio of embroideries. The flowers are a delight and add such a touch of elegance to these linens.

"Machines can never put art into an object. Only hands and hearts can do that."
HOME ARTS (October 1937)

scalloped wreath pattern on pages 64-65
daisies tied in a bow pattern on pages 70-71
poppies in a basket pattern on pages 68-69

Appealing Apron

Before today's easy wash-and-wear lifestyle, aprons played a much larger role in the lives of women. Besides protecting dresses, they added a flare to fashions. Both formal and utilitarian aprons were decorated and nothing brought a hostess more compliments than a tastefully done apron to match her frock!

daisies in a basket pattern on pages 66-67

Doilies and Scarves

"There is always just the place for an odd doily; it serves to hold a bon-bon dish, a bowl of flowers, a bit of china or bric-a-brac, and in a half hundred different ways. And so we can never have too many, or in too generous variety".
NEEDLECRAFT (May 1925)

single flower pattern on pages 75
double flower pattern on pages 74-75
large scarf pattern on pages 72-73

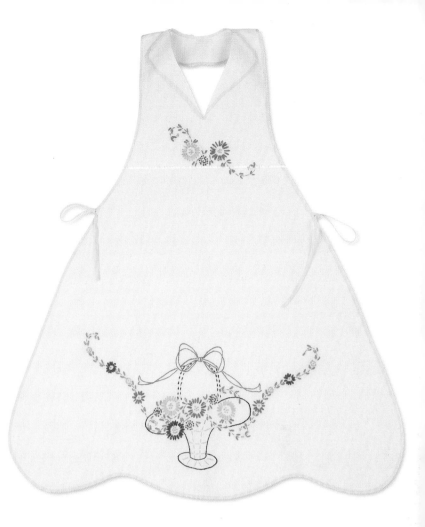

Pillow Talk

Pillows have been a standard decoration in homes for many years. Victorians were especially fond of elaborately decorated pillows in abundance. This trend continued over the years and a great variety of pillow patterns and kits appeared throughout needlework catalogs.

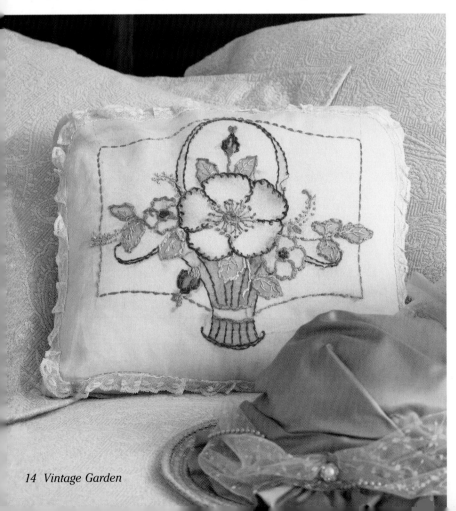

A Tisket, A Tasket, What a Pretty Basket!

Variegated floss produces dazzling effects, allowing you to embroider baskets and flowers with soft, subtle shadings that look so real!

The black basket with flowers is a prime example of 1920s embroidery designs. The intricate basket detail and the abundance of flowers in subtle hues was a popular design motif of that period. This lovely pillow, formerly a table runner, is a good example of using lovely older linens for something other than they were intended. It's a good way to display stitchery.

The vintage brown basket pillow with the blue outline border was a preprinted design. The fabric was already shaded in the basket, handle, leaves and flower edges, so the stitcher only had to embroider the outlines to create a beautiful piece of art.

The tinted basket with simple lines and uncomplicated flowers is more reminiscent of the 1930s. Tinting was first popular in the 1920s and continued through the middle 1940s when it suddenly became absent in catalogs. What a misfortune! There is nothing as nostalgic and charming as tinted needlework. It lends a certain charm that is hard to imitate with other techniques. This is a perfect opportunity to use this design and tinting techniques described in this book to create your own little bit of yesteryear.

black basket pattern on pages 76-77
brown basket pattern on pages 78-79

blue basket pattern on page 84
basket on shaped brown linen
pattern on pages 80-81
gold basket pattern on pages 82-83

Baskets, Butterflies and Bows

What a delight to find tables full of flowers! While table linens are once again coming into vogue with antique collectors and needleworkers alike, this is a good chance to capture your own bit of history.

bows pattern on page 85
blue flowers in a basket pattern on pages 86-87
butterflies and basket pattern on pages 94-95

Tempting Table Linens

These linens are gorgeous and very intricate but like most lovely things are worth the time and are truly a labor of love. Choosing colors carefully lets these tablecloths complement any decor and give you that "designer" look.

flower border patterns on pages 90-91
cornucopia pattern on pages 92-93
basket of spider web flowers
pattern on pages 88-89

Brocade Wall Quilt

Magic Blocks...

Old tablecloths and bridge sets are lovely to look at but are not as relevant to today's lifestyle and entertainment. One great way to enjoy the lovely handwork and labor that went into these old treasures is to recycle them into something very popular today – quilts and wall hangings. Since many old cloths were arranged with similar designs gracing the corner, it's just a simple matter of rearranging these into on-point quilt blocks. If you have corner designs which can be cut into square blocks, simply work these with borders into a quilt.

basket patterns on pages 20 - 21

Brocade Wall Quilt

FINISHED SIZE: 63" x 63"

FABRICS:
- 1 yard White for embroidered center squares
- ⅔ yard Green for corner triangles
- ⅙ yard Plaid for bias trim
- 2 yards Brown for borders and binding
- ⅔ yard Red for middle borders
- 1¾ yards backing 90" wide
  - or piece the back from scraps to make a 64" square

MATERIALS:
- Embroidery floss
- Embroidery needle size 8

CUTTING:
Quilt center:
- 4 White 16" squares for the embroidered blocks
- 3 Green 14½" squares; cut 2 on 1 diagonal, making 4 triangles
- 2 Green 10½" squares for corners of the embroidered blocks;
  - cut each block on 1 diagonal, making 4 triangles
- 4 strips Plaid bias 1¼" x 40½"

Inner Brown border:
- Top/bottom strips 2" x 40½"
- 2 side strips 2" x 43½"

Middle Red border:
- Top/bottom strips 4" x 43½"
- 2 side strips 4" x 50½"

Outer Brown border:
- Top/bottom strips 6½" x 50½"
- 2 side strips 6½" x 62½"

Brown backing:
- 1 square 64" x 64"

Binding:
- Brown 2½" strips sewn together to make 255" (7 yards, 3")

INSTRUCTIONS:
1. Trace the pattern onto each White block. Embroider. Press.
   Trim square to 14½" x 14½".
2. Row 1: Sew 2 Green 14½" triangles to each side of the embroidered block.
   Row 2: Sew an embroidered block, 14½" Green square, and another embroidered block together.
   Row 3: Sew 2 Green 14½" triangles to each side of the embroidered block.
3. Sew the Green triangle corner blocks in place to make a center 40½" x 40½".
4. Fold and press each bias Plaid strip in half lengthwise ⅝" x 40½".
   Pin and sew it to the edge of the center 4-Patch with a seam slightly smaller than ¼" so the seam will be hidden by the border seam allowance.
5. Brown Inner Border: Sew the top and bottom to the quilt. Press.
   Sew the sides to the quilt. Press.
6. Red Middle Border: Sew the top and bottom to the quilt. Press.
   Sew the sides to the quilt. Press.
7. Brown Outer Border: Sew the top and bottom to the quilt. Press.
   Sew the sides to the quilt. Press.
8. Layer backing, batting and top to form a sandwich.
   Baste the layers together. Quilt as desired.
   Trim the backing and batting to the edge of the quilt top.
9. Sew binding strips into one long piece.
   Press binding in half lengthwise.
   Sew binding to the quilt front.
   Turn to the back and hem by hand.

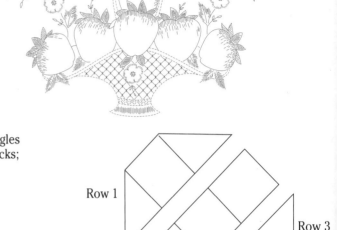

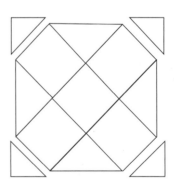

Row 1
Row 2
Row 3

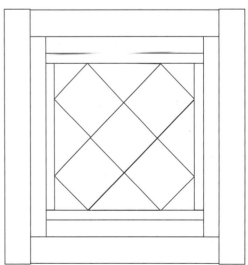

Assembly Diagram

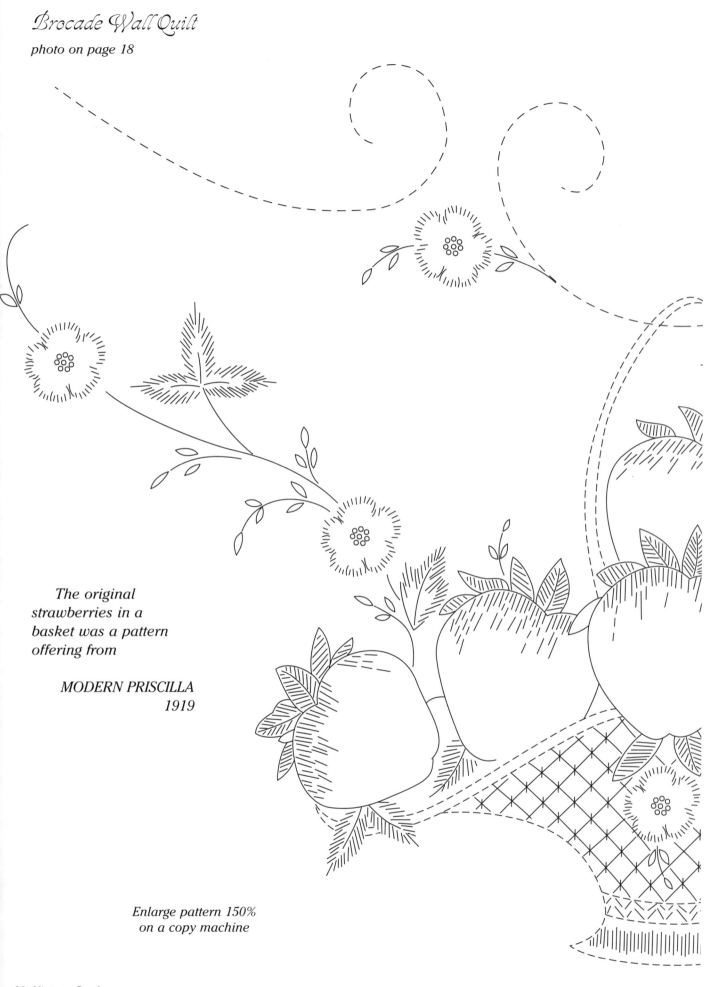

The original
strawberries in a
basket was a pattern
offering from

MODERN PRISCILLA
1919

Enlarge pattern 150%
on a copy machine

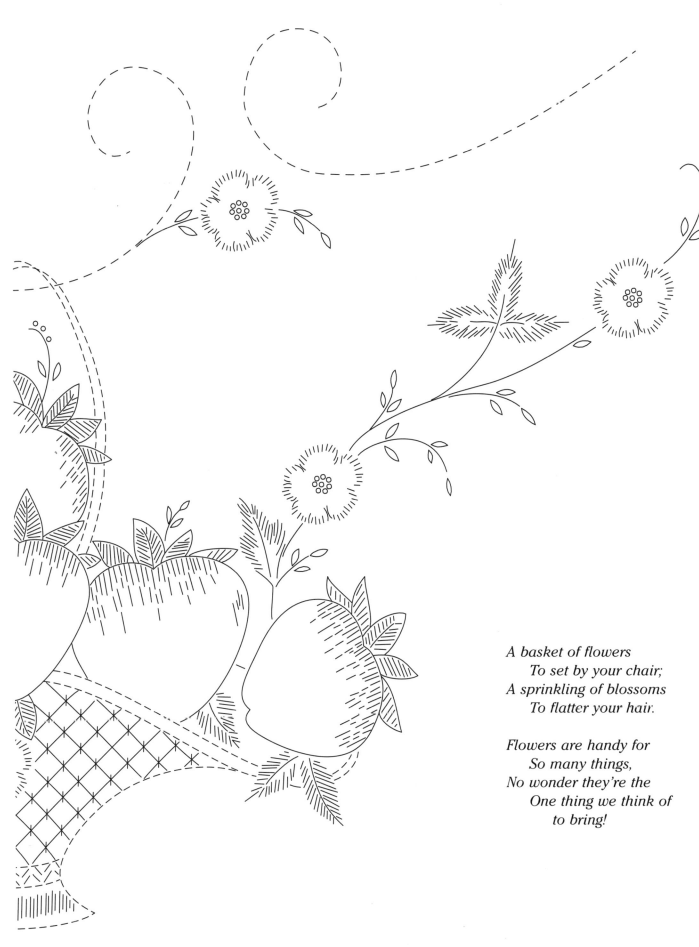

A basket of flowers
    To set by your chair;
A sprinkling of blossoms
    To flatter your hair.

Flowers are handy for
    So many things,
No wonder they're the
    One thing we think of
        to bring!

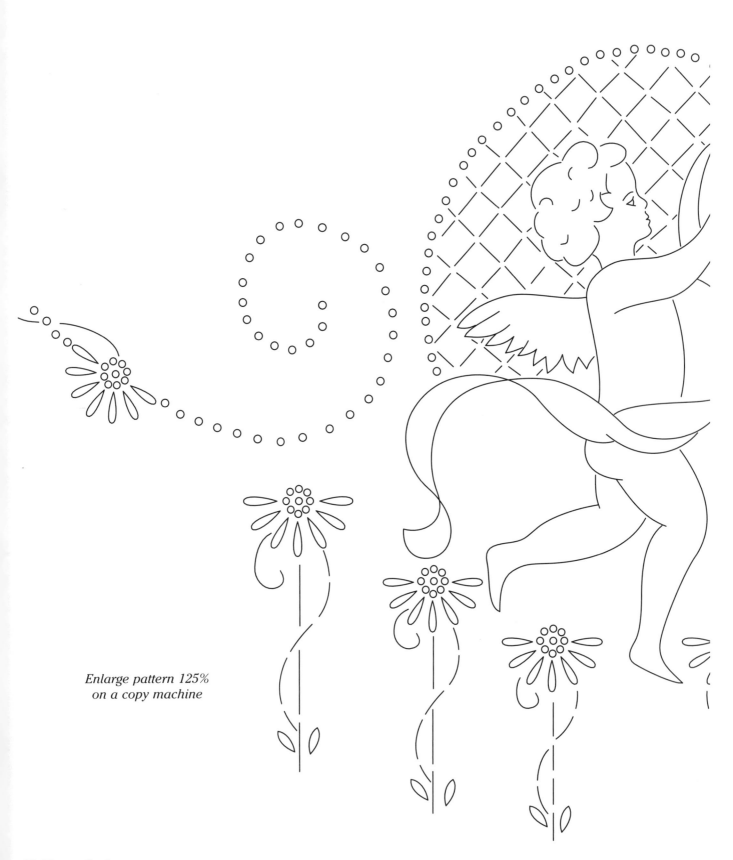

*Enlarge pattern 125%
on a copy machine*

A lovely way to pass a day
NEEDLECRAFT
September 1926

Rose Bouquet in a Black Vase
photo on page 3

*Enlarge pattern 125%
on a copy machine*

Pansies in a Fan Basket

photo on page 3

_Enlarge pattern 125%
on a copy machine_

Garden Girls

BY MARY CAROLYN DAVIES

GIRLS who walk in gardens wear
   A fragrant halo on their hair.
Girls whose fingers know the graces
Of sweet peas, whose eager faces
Have long felt the petals of
Rose and violet, girls who love
Honeysuckle, phlox, and pink,
Peony, pansy, girls who drink
Hearty draughts of sweetness up
From a yellow lily cup,
Girls who walk in gardens, keep
All the sweet of gardens, deep
In their eyes and hearts, to bring
Garden peace and comforting
To all those who have forgot
To tend, themselves, a garden plot.

Red Flowers in a Basket

photo on page 2

*Enlarge pattern 125%
on a copy machine*

Care of Linens

Washing -

• Test for colorfastness on the seam allowance. Let several drops of water fall through the fabric onto white blotter paper. If color appears, the fabric is not colorfast.

• To set dye, soak fabric in water and vinegar.

• Wash with a very mild detergent or soap, using tepid water. Follow all label instructions carefully.

• Do not use chlorine bleach on fine linen. Whiten it by hanging it in full sunlight.

Stain Removal -

• Grease - Use a presoak fabric treatment and wash in cold water.

• Non-greasy - Soak in cold water to neutralize the stain. Apply a presoak and then wash in cold water.

• Ballpoint Ink - Place on an absorbent material and soak with denatured or rubbing alcohol. Apply room temperature glycerin and flush with water. Finally, apply ammonia and quickly flush with water.

• Candle Wax - Place fabric between layers of absorbent paper and iron on low setting. Change paper as it absorbs wax. If a stain remains, wash with peroxide bleach.

• Rust - Remove with lemon juice, oxalic acid or hydrofluoric acid.

Storage -

• Wash and rinse thoroughly in soft water.

• Do not size or starch.

• Place cleaned linen on acid-free tissue paper and roll loosely.

• Line storage boxes with a layer of acid-free tissue paper.

• Place rolled linens in a box. Do not stack. Weight causes creases in the fabric.

• Do not store linens in plastic bags.

• Hang linen clothing in a muslin bag or cover with a cotton sheet.

Enlarge pattern 125%
on a copy machine

Young Age Passion
    by Ethel Romig Fuller

It cannot be bought,
    Nor may it be sold,
Though coveted more
    Than jewels and gold;

Nor borrowed, nor pawned,
    Nor even lent –
Youth's honey-bright treasure
    May only be spent.

HOME ARTS
May 1940

Enlarge pattern 125%
on a copy machine

Pitcher and Bowl

photo on page 4

Pattern is full size

Design on back

This little fellow's worked so hard
To bring his load to you,
So thank the hardy donkey
It's the least that we could do!

Pattern is full size

Spray Bouquet
photo on page 5

What a treat! This I don't mind,
*   It can storm away.*
Where else can you fill your vase,
*   On a rainy day!*

Pattern is full size

Parasol

photo on page 5

*Careful there it's raining out
Put your 'brella up.
But wait, it's not as bad as it seems,
It's raining buttercups.*

Pattern is full size

Nasturtiums

BY EDITH D. OSBORNE

Flame flowers, orange and amber,
  Crimson, scarlet and gold;
Petals like butterflies' anchored wings
  Ruffled and curled and rolled.

Clean and sharp is the fragrance
  That comes from the heart of them,
Each little sunshine blossom
  Cupped on its slim green stem.

No matter how poor the soil is
  With many a rock between,
They cover the ground with their glory
  In a carpet of brightest green.

From early summer till winter's frost
  They linger, valiant and true,
Flame flowers, honey and amber,
  Loyal the whole year through.

Pattern is full size

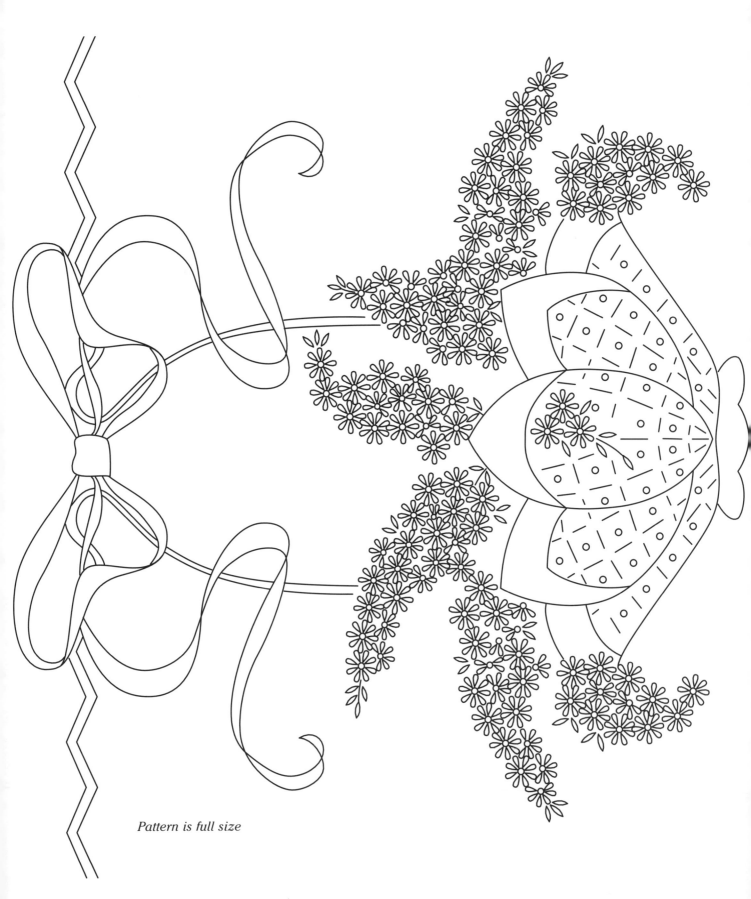

Pattern is full size

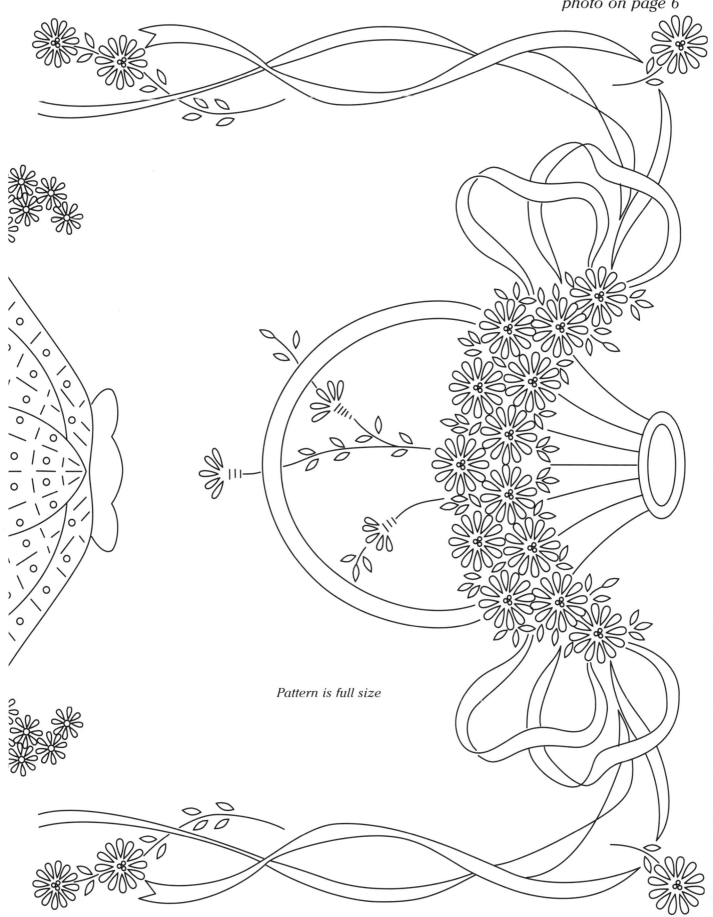

Pattern is full size

Heart and Roses
photo on page 6

November, 1924

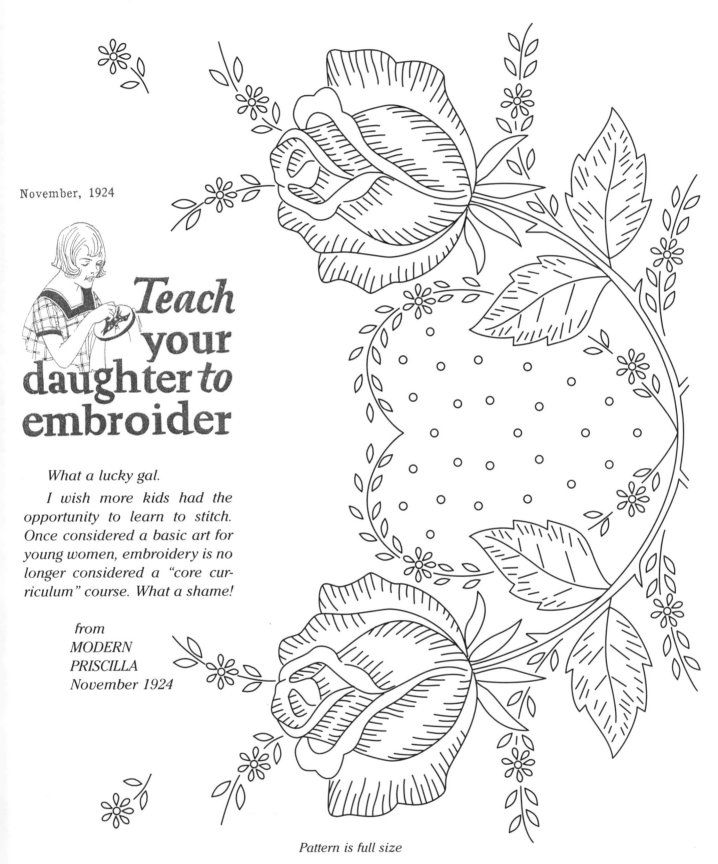

Teach your daughter *to* embroider

What a lucky gal.

I wish more kids had the opportunity to learn to stitch. Once considered a basic art for young women, embroidery is no longer considered a "core curriculum" course. What a shame!

from
MODERN
PRISCILLA
November 1924

Pattern is full size

Pattern is full size

Tiny Basket and Bouquets

photo on page 6

Pattern is full size

THE ROSE SCHOOL

BY CELIA THORNTON

Mistress Pink Rose keeps a school
In the garden, leafy, cool;
Teaches rosebuds how to grow,
How to dance when south
    winds blow,

How to curtsy, how to dress
With the most becomingness.
When the summer school term
    closes,
    Pupils all are perfect
        roses.

DRAWN BY
L. J. BRIDGMAN

DRAWN BY MAY AIKEN

THE ROSE

By MARY STANTON
BOUTWELL

Priscilla in
        the garden
In a quaint gown,
Priscilla in
        the garden
And the sun
        looking down—

She stood so very quiet,
She did not
        move or speak,
But smiled a
        little, faintly,
With a dimple
        in her cheek.

All round about her
The leaves were
        very green;
She was the
        sweetest thing
The sun had
        ever seen.

Will somebody
        tell me,
If anybody knows,
If at first the
        sun suspected
Priscilla was a rose?

This is an ad for items offered by Bucilla.
MODERN PRISCILLA
November 1924

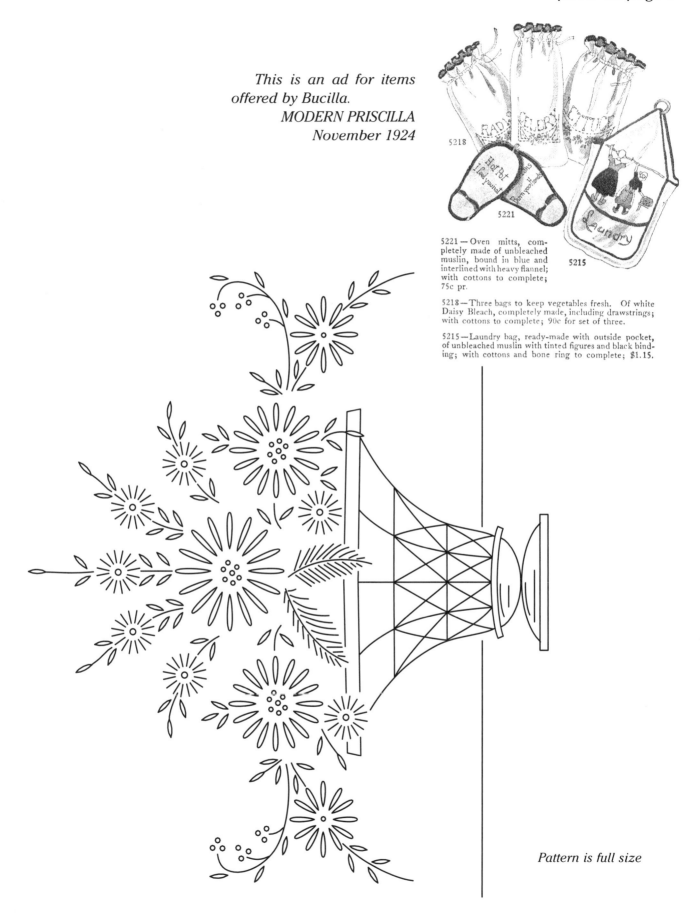

5218

5221

5215

5221 — Oven mitts, completely made of unbleached muslin, bound in blue and interlined with heavy flannel; with cottons to complete; 75c pr.

5218 — Three bags to keep vegetables fresh. Of white Daisy Bleach, completely made, including drawstrings; with cottons to complete; 90c for set of three.

5215 — Laundry bag, ready-made with outside pocket, of unbleached muslin with tinted figures and black binding; with cottons and bone ring to complete; $1.15.

Pattern is full size

Beribboned Basket

photo on page 7

Wonder what they're saying?

MODERN PRISCILLA
February 1913

Pattern is full size

Kitty
photo on page 8

Who's that peeking from the weeds?
    It's my clever cat.
He's playing hide and seek with me.
    Can you imagine that?

He'll come home by dinner time.
    He's never missed a meal.
Play all day and hurry home,
    This kitty's got a deal!

Pattern is full size

Wouldn't you love to order these items? They were available in 1924.

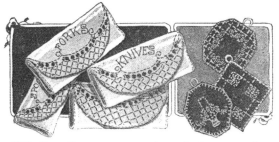

Purple Wreaths

photo on page 9

Pattern is full size

Roses

photo on page 9

Borders to wrap your pillow in
And trim your dreams with color,
What better way to go to sleep –
Next to a lovely flower.

Pattern is full size

Flower Wreath
photo on page 8

Darling Deer
photo on page 10

Pattern is full size

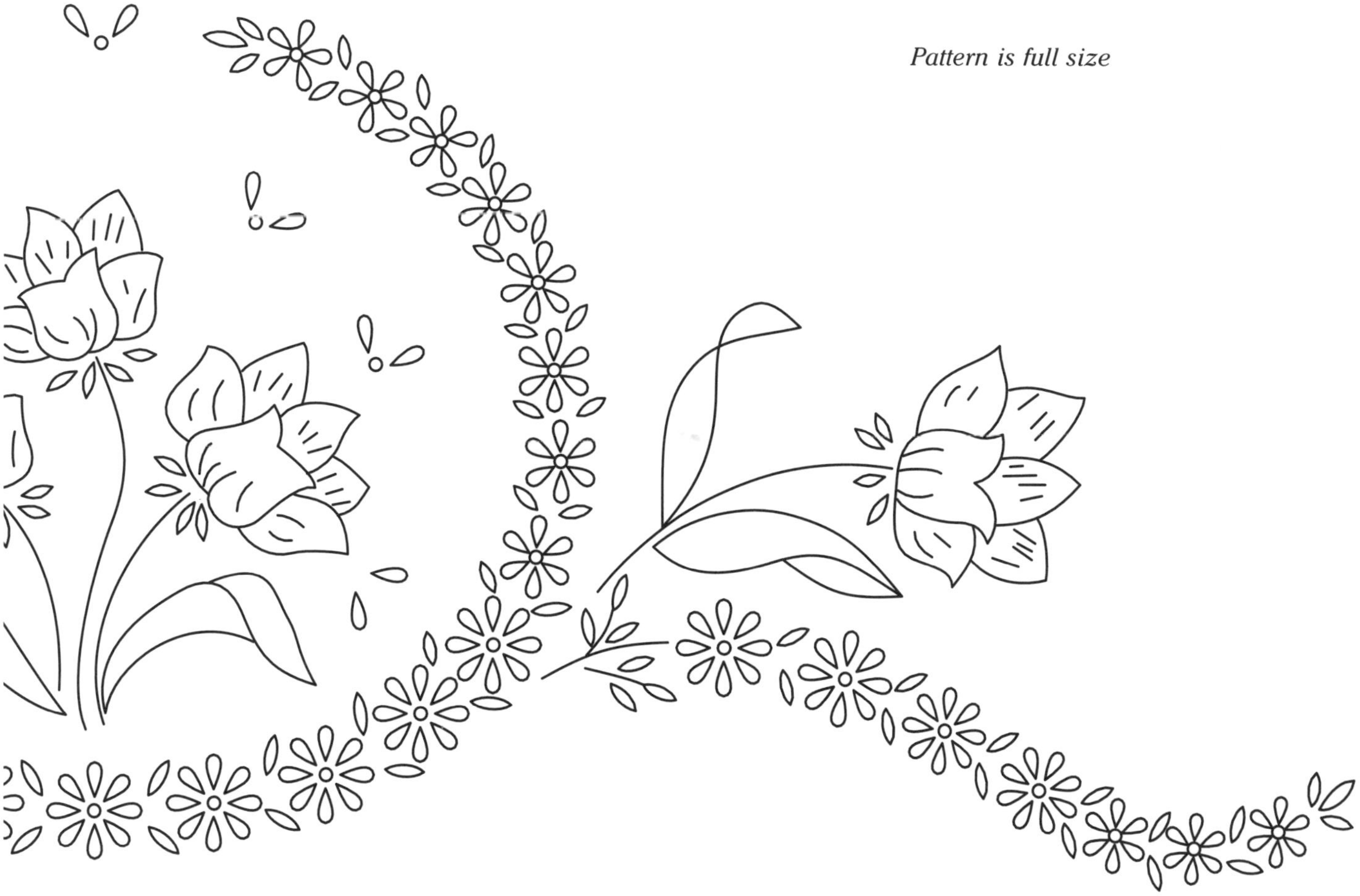

Pattern is full size

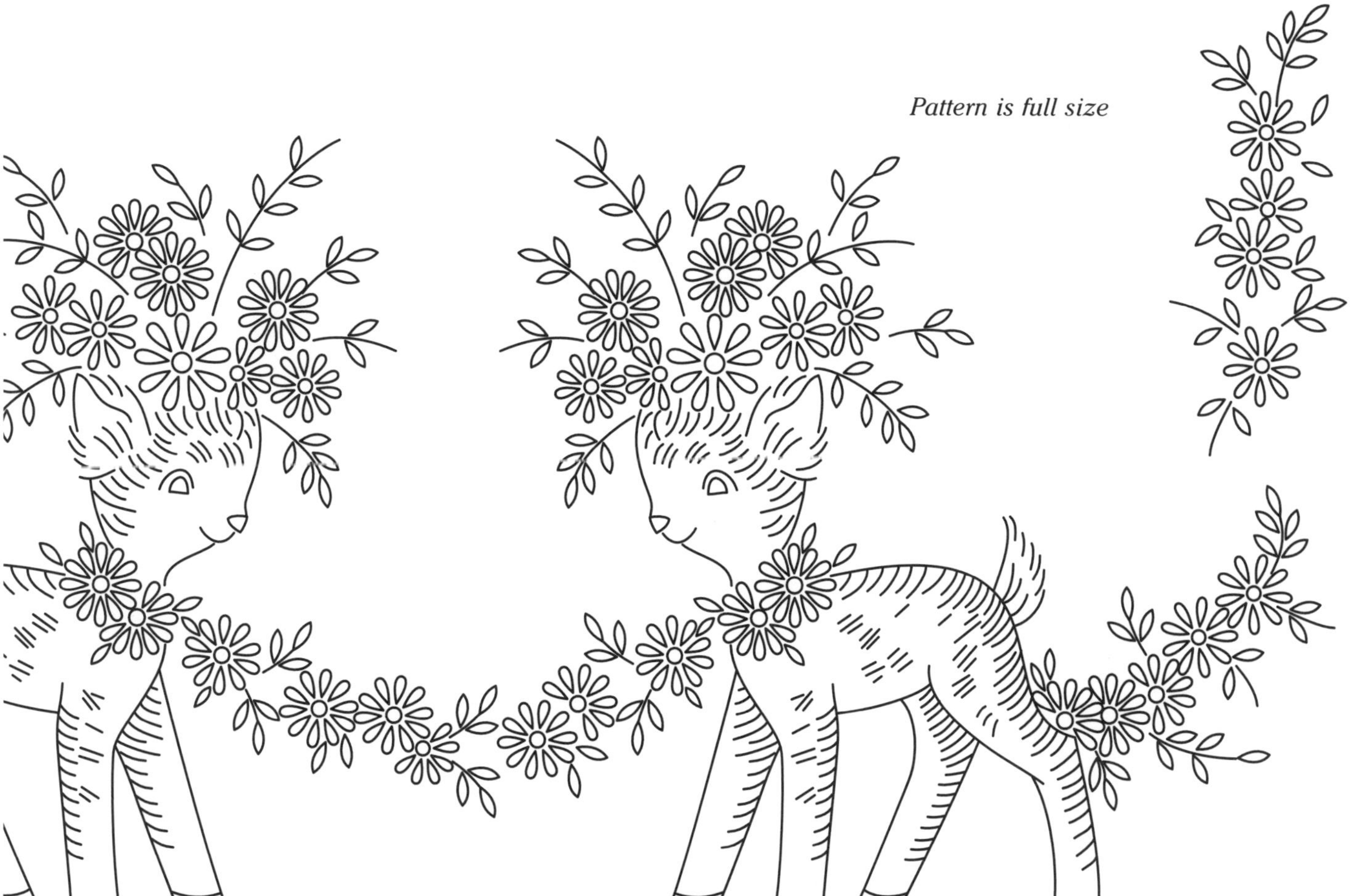

Good Luck
photo on page 8

"It is recreation, truly, to spend a happy hour or two with a piece of embroidery or other favorite fancywork – which is useful too – in hand, placing the stitches and watching the design grow under one's fingers...."

NEEDLECRAFT
September 1925

Pattern is full size

This gal better keep her mind on what she's doing. A mouth full of pins can be quite dangerous.

Clipping from
MODERN PRISCILLA
October 1919

Flowers and Bows
photo on page 9

Heart and Flowers
photo on page 9

Basket of Lilacs

photo on page 10

Assembly Diagram

A basket of lilacs to grace my table
    Can cheer me more than most are able.
They brighten the house
    And scent the air,
You know they'll look perfect
    Anywhere.

Pattern is full size

Cornucopia
photo on page 9

Pattern is full size

Magnolias
photo on page 10

Pattern is full size

d BRUSH

Pattern is full size

Grapes
photo
on page 11

Pattern is full size

Pay attention to backgrounds.

When working with lighter-colored fabrics, do not carry dark flosses across large unworked background areas. Stop and start again to prevent unsightly 'ghost strings' from showing through the front.

Another option is to back tinted muslin with another layer of muslin before you add embroidery stitches. This will help keep 'ghost strings' from showing.

Lazy Daisy Stitch

Come up at A. Go down at B (right next to A) to form a loop. Come back up at C with the needle tip over the thread. Go down at D to make a small anchor stitch over the top of the loop.

Running Stitch

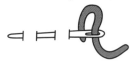

Come up at A. Weave the needle through the fabric, making short, even stitches. Use this stitch to gather fabrics, too.

Satin Stitch

Work small straight stitches close together and at the same angle to fill an area with stitches. Vary the length of the stitches as required to keep the outline of the area smooth.

Stem Stitch

Work from left to right to make regular, slanting stitches along the stitch line. Bring the needle up above the center of the last stitch. Also called 'Outline' stitch.

Straight Stitch

Come up at A and go down at B to form a simple flat stitch. Use this stitch for hair for animals and for simple petals on small flowers.

Whip Stitch

Insert the needle under a few fibers of one layer of fabric. Bring the needle up through the other layer of fabric. Use this stitch to attach the folded raw edges of fabric to the back of pieces or to attach bindings around the edges of quilts and coverlets.

Embroidery Stitches

Working with Floss. Separate embroidery floss.

Use 24" lengths of floss and a #8 embroidery needle.

Use 2 to 3 ply floss to outline large elements of the design and to embroider larger and more stylized patterns.

Use 2 ply for the small details on some items.

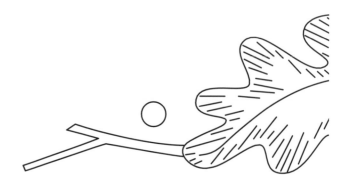

Blanket Stitch

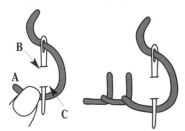

Come up at A, hold the thread down with your thumb, go down at B. Come back up at C with the needle tip over the thread. Pull the stitch into place. Repeat, outlining with the bottom legs of the stitch. Use this stitch to edge fabrics.

Acorns and Oak Leaves
photo on page 11

Chain Stitch

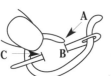 

Come up at A. To form a loop, hold the thread down with your thumb, go down at B (as close as possible to A). Come back up at C with the needle tip over the thread. Repeat to form a chain.

Cross Stitch

 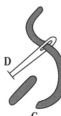

Make a diagonal Straight stitch (up at A, down at B) from upper right to lower left. Come up at C and go down at D to make another diagonal Straight stitch the same length as the first one. The stitch will form an X.

French Knot

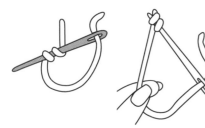

Come up at A. Wrap the floss around the needle 2 to 3 times. Insert the needle close to A. Hold the floss and pull the needle through the loops gently.

Herringbone Stitch

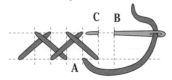 

Come up at A. Make a slanted stitch to the top right, inserting the needle at B. Come up a short distance away at C.

Insert the needle at D to complete the stitch. Bring the needle back up at the next A to begin a new stitch. Repeat.

A little house beside the road
A garden by its side
Makes one yearn to return home
And behind its door I'll hide.

Pattern is full size

Star Flower
photo on page 11

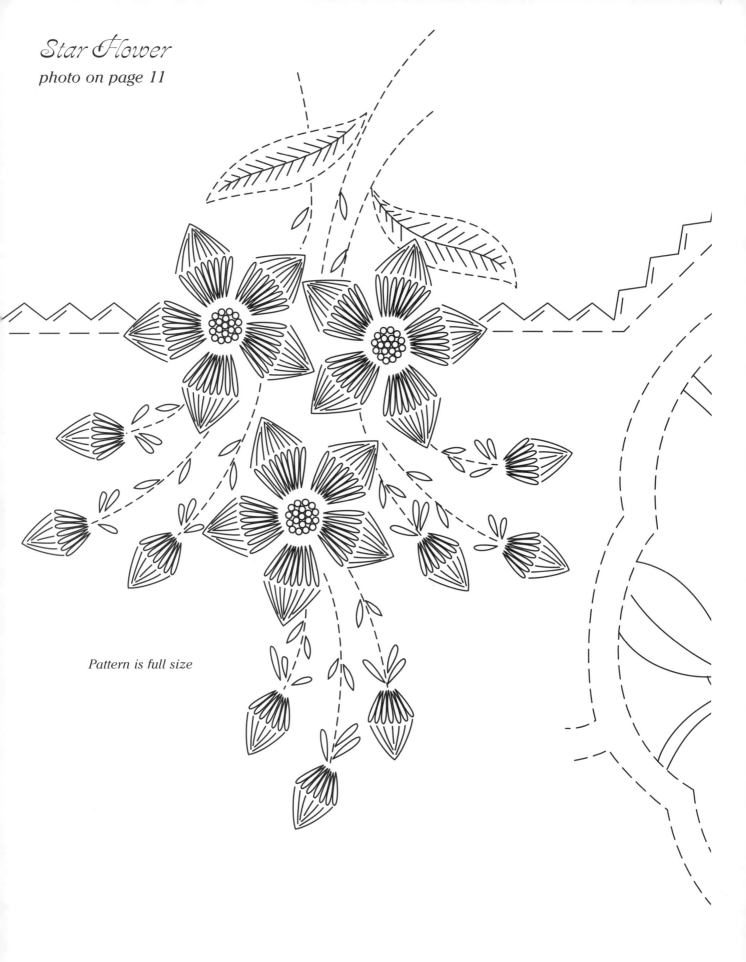

Pattern is full size

Pattern is full size

Daisies in a Basket

photo on page 13

*Enlarge pattern 125%
on a copy machine*

Poppies in a Basket
photo on page 12

Clipping from NEEDLECRAFT
January 1927

A stitch in time...

Pattern is full size

Half a dozen Daisies tied in a Bow

photo on page 12

Patience my dear!

MODERN PRISCILLA
October 1924

Clipping from MODERN PRISCILLA
April 1923

Pattern is full size

*Enlarge pattern 125%
on a copy machine*

Double Flower
photo on page 13

Pattern is full size

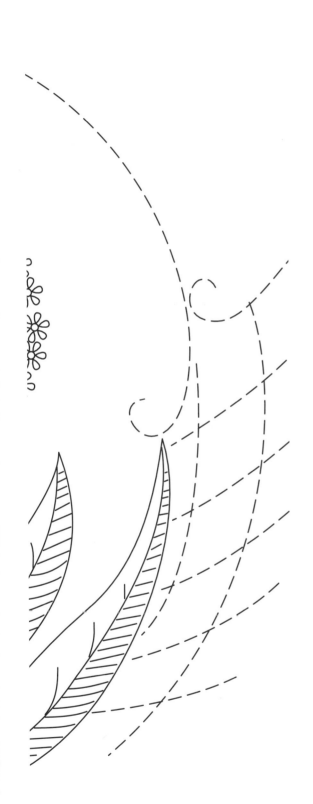

Black Basket with Flowers

photo on page 14

Pattern is full size

Pattern is full size

Basket on Brown Linen

photo on page 15

*Enlarge pattern 125%
on a copy machine*

Sooner or later everything gets done!

MODERN PRISCILLA
October 1924

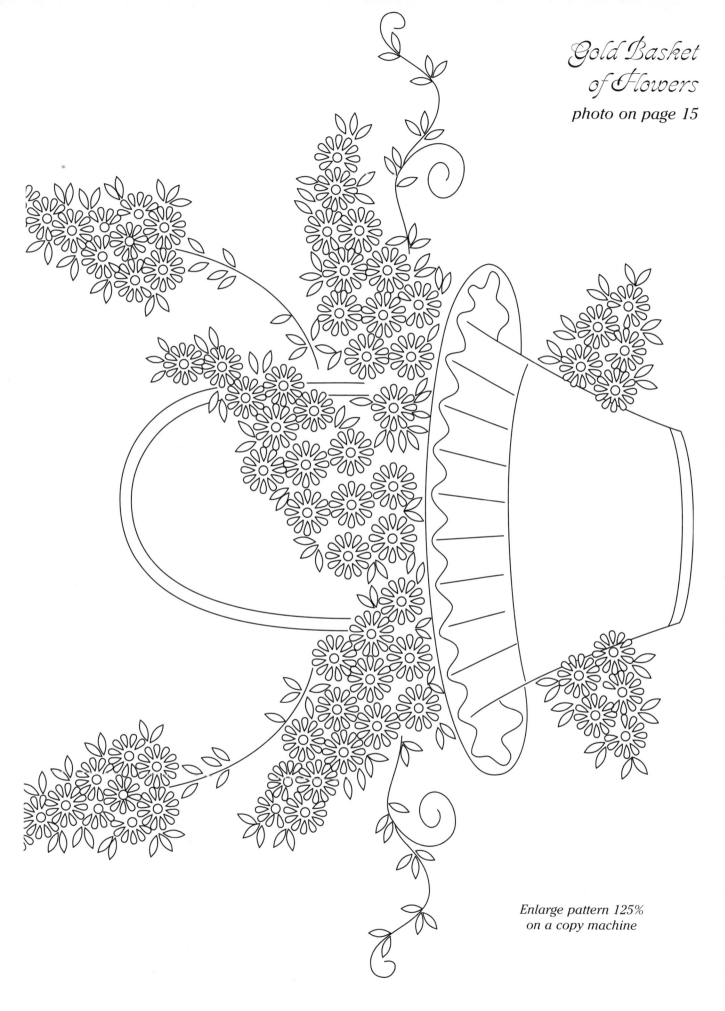

Enlarge pattern 125%
on a copy machine

Pattern is full size

Pattern is full size

Blue Flowers in a Basket

photo on page 16

Pattern is full size

Someone has to grow them!

HOME ARTS
1938

Basket of Spider Web Flowers

photo on page 17

Instructions for Spoke Flowers

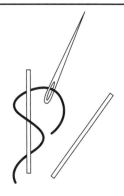
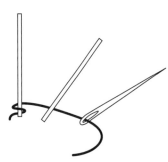
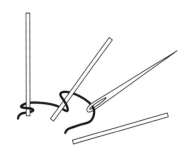

Take thread under spoke, back to left side, and under spoke again.

Pull back against bottom of spoke; take needle and thread under next spoke.

Repeat around the entire circle.

How to Embroider a Spoke Wheel

Sew a long stitch to make each spoke of the wheel.

Bring the thread out on the right side of the spoke next to the center point.

Slide the needle under the spoke from left to right. Do Not pierce the fabric.

Slide the needle under the spoke again to wrap the spoke.

Pull the threads gently along the spoke toward the center.

Bring the needle under the next spoke on the right.

Slide the needle under the second spoke, and wrap just like you did for the first spoke.

Repeat until you have covered all the spokes.

To change thread, knot off in the back, and begin where you left off with the previous thread.

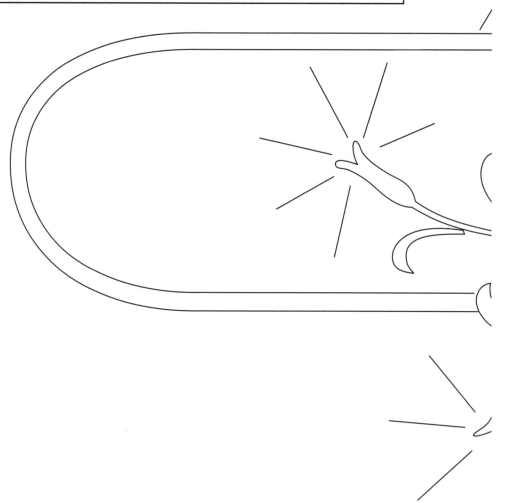

*Enlarge pattern 125%
on a copy machine*

Flower Border
photo on page 17

Premium No. B 1792   Given for Five Subscriptions

Pattern is full size

Cornucopia
photo on page 17

Stitching

    by Christina G. Rosetti

A pocket handkerchief to hem
    Oh dear, oh dear, oh dear!
How many stitches will it take
    Before it's done I fear.

You set a stitch and
    then a stitch,
And stitch and
    stitch away,
'Til stitch by stitch,
    the hem is done,
And after work is play!

      LADIES' HOME JOURNAL
          August 1907

Pattern is full size

Butterflies and Basket
photo on page 16

*Enlarge pattern 150%
on a copy machine*

Enlarge pattern 150%
on a copy machine

Floral Quilt
photo on page 18

FINISHED SIZE: 75" x 96"

FABRICS:

2¼ yards White for embroidered squares, square-in-a-square blocks, triangle border, and binding

½ yard Yellow for square-in-a-square blocks

3½ yards each Blue and Pink for pieced rectangles

2¾ yards 90" wide fabric for the backing

MATERIALS:

Embroidery floss

Embroidery needle size 8

CUTTING & CONSTRUCTION:

Embroidery:

Cut 12 White 17" squares for the embroidered blocks

Trace the pattern onto each White block. Embroider. Press.

Trim blocks to 16½" square.

Square in a Square:

Cut 20 White 5½" squares.

Draw the lines of the inner square on all 20 squares using the drawing as a guide.

Cut 40 Yellow 3¼" squares. Cut each Yellow square on 1 diagonal.

Follow the diagram to position the Yellow square to form each corner.

Sew a ¼" seam that covers the line you drew.

Flip the Yellow triangle back and press.

Repeat for all Yellow triangles on all White squares.

Rectangle Blocks:

All rectangle blocks are made the same way. See Rectangle Block Diagrams.

If you stack these strips following the diagrams, you will get pairs of rectangles that are not the same.

This is important to notice. For example, look at row 1.

The horizontal rectangles have the diagonals going in different directions.

To get the overall design to come out right, you must pay attention to the placement of the color as well as the direction of the diagonal.

Stack Blue fabric right side up. The orientation of the fabric is important.

Stack Pink fabric also right side up.

Cut 31 stacked rectangles 6½" x 16½".

Draw and cut on 1 diagonal.

See diagram to get the orientation of the triangles so they fit together.

Pin the bias edge and sew.

Press the block open. Trim to 5½" x 16½"

continued on page 98

**Square-in-a-Square
White and Yellow Corners**

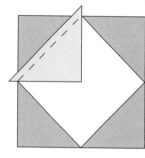

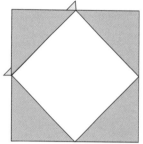

Pink and Blue Rectangles:

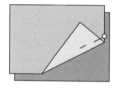
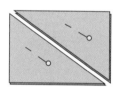
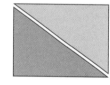
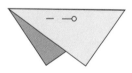

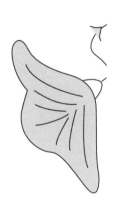

Floral Quilt

continued from page 96

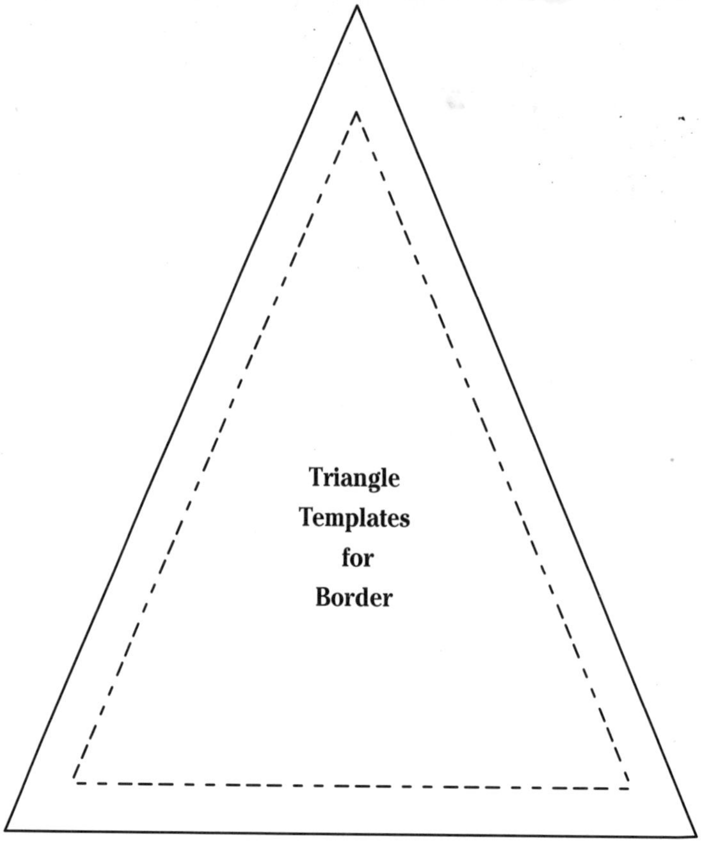

BACKING:
Cut or piece 1 rectangle 77" x 98".

BINDING:
Cut 8 White 2½" x 44" strips. Sew together to make 345" (9⅝ yards).

ASSEMBLY:

Follow the Assembly Diagram.

Sew the blocks together to form rows. Press. Sew the rows together. Press.

Triangle Border:

You will need 105 White, 53 Pink and 52 Blue triangles.

Cut 7 White strips 4½" x 44".

Cut 4 strips of Blue and 4 strips of Pink 4½" x 44".

If you stack these strips, you can cut out the triangles using the template.

Use the Border Assembly

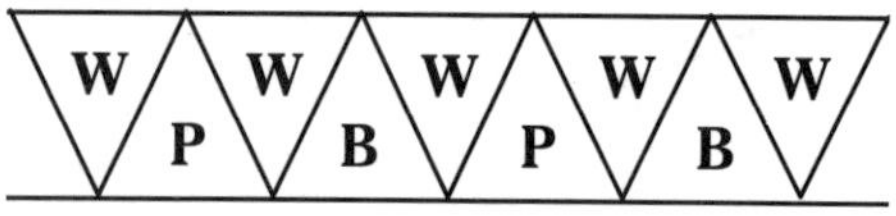

Diagram to sew a string of alternating triangles to fit the perimeter of the quilt.

You will have to adjust your triangle size to turn the corner for your quilt.

FINISH:

Layer backing, batting and top to form a sandwich. Baste the layers together.

Quilt as desired. Trim the backing and batting to the edge of the quilt top.

Press binding in half lengthwise. Using a ¼" seam allowance, sew binding to the quilt front.

Turn to the back and hem by hand.

HELPFUL HINT
See Embroidery Stitches on pages 61 and 62.

MANY THANKS to my friends for their cheerful help and wonderful ideas!
Kathy McMillan • Jennifer Laughlin
Janie Ray • Janet Long
Patty Williams • Marti Wyble
Donna Kinsey
David & Donna Thomason

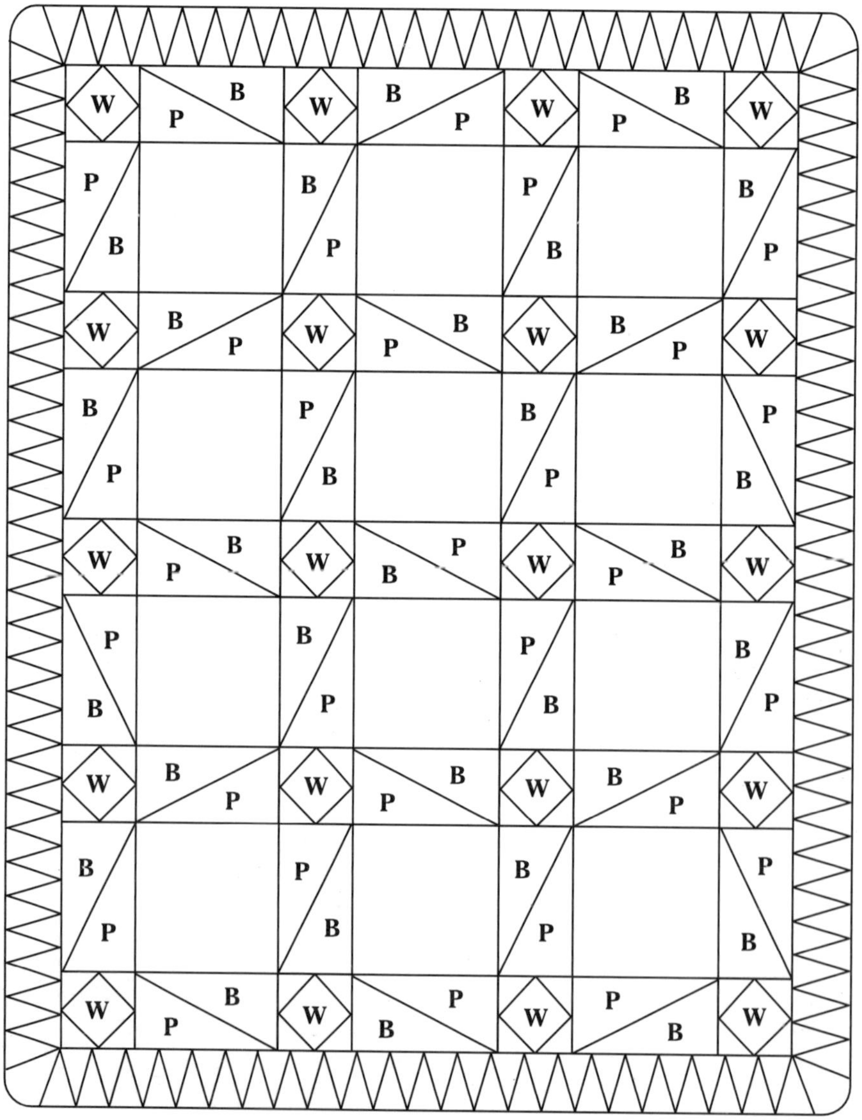